50 Ways To Be An Effective Father

The Black Man's Guide To Parenting

C.F. Gipson

THE BLACK MAN'S GUIDE TO PARENTING. Copyright ©2006 by Constance F. Gipson

Publisher's Cataloging-in-Publication
(Provided by Quality Books, Inc.)

Gipson, C. F. (Constance F.)
   The black man's guide to parenting : 50 ways to be an
effective father / by C.F. Gipson.
      p. cm.
   ISBN 1-883423-11-2
   1. Fatherhood--United States. 2. African American
fathers. 3. Child rearing--United States. 4. African
American families.   I. Title.
   HQ756.G545 2006   306.874'2'08996073
                             QBI06-600008

Edited by Cathy Feldman
Design by Penelope C. Paine and Cathy Feldman
Book Production by Blue Point Books

Cover photograph by Patricia Lutfy
Photography credits: Page 42 - Harris Studio, Sacramento, CA

ISBN-13: 978-1-883423-11-7
ISBN 10: 1-883423-11-2

First Edition
10 9 8 7 6 5 4 3 2 1

Published by Blue Point Books
P.O. Box 91347
Santa Barbara, CA 93190-1347
800-858-1058
bpbooks@west.net • www.bluepointbooks.com

Dedication

For black fathers who have custody, joint custody,
are non-custodial parents, and
for the millions of black male parents who,
throughout history, have stayed.

Acknowledgements

I am grateful for the advice, support and encouragement from the following people:

Rena Bancroft, Gloria and Angela Blanchette, Sarah and Harold Boyd, Katherine Crowder, Robert and Darrien Dorn, Ellen Duke, Sue Estes, Irvin and Evelyn Gipson, Irvin Mitchell Gipson, Jr., Jarvio and Lucinda Grevious, Kamilah Jackson, Deidre and Shawn Henry, Bobbie and Lawrence Jones, George and Kathy King, Hazel Mahone, Robert and Loretta Mathews, Martha McDowell, Anthony Milton, Carolyn and Cordell Olive, Peggy and Laura Olivier, Penny Paine, Kenneth and Allyson Gipson Pettway, Lillian Robinson, Kevin Smith, Willa Mae and Allison Smith, Sarah Taylor, Evelyn and Carlon Thompson, Cora Thompson, Burl and Jodi Thornton, Victor and Hazel Thornton, Burl Toler, Samuel and Em Johns Vaughn, Paul Watkins, Doris Ward, Karen Ward, Brenda Williams, James Williams, David and Patricia Wood and Amber Wynn.

Introduction

Today's black children face fierce competition. As a black parent, you might not have faced the Asians, whites, Latinos, and immigrant students who are competing against black students today.

Many of these students come from two-parent homes and from well-maintained schools that have competent teachers and superior resources. They have parents who have provided them with many extra learning activities, private tutors, enrichment camps, trips to museums and libraries, and trips to college campuses. These parents have provided computers and have read to their children from their earliest years. Many of them have entered their children in the best pre-schools and have delayed their entrance into kindergarten because older mature students tend to do better than young immature students. They encourage their children to spend their time in summer school and take advantage of learning centers like Sylvan and Kaplan. Their children have received the message that they are going to college. Their children have been to concerts and the theater, visited historical sites, and their homes are filled with reading material. Some parents see repeating a grade not as a punishment or failure but a strategy to improve scores later on. These parents spend time selecting a school where they think their children will do well and buy homes in those neighborhoods.

Today's black children face problems that their grandparents and parents did not have. The grandparents of today's black children often lived in segregated neighborhoods and went to all-black schools. Due to segregation, educated and non-educated, well-to-do and poor blacks lived together in these neighborhoods. Black children were exposed to successful blacks and were urged to prepare themselves for the days when more opportunities would become available to them.

Black communities and churches sponsored programs where children would shine and develop their skills in oratory, drama and music. Black children went to schools that had demanding principals and teachers. Even though their facilities were sometimes less attractive than white schools and their textbooks were old and obsolete, the children learned to read and do mathematics. They were exhorted to work hard because they had to be "twice as good as whites" to succeed. They were taught they had an obligation to their ancestors and elders to do well. They were taught Negro history, told about black heroes, and told to have pride in being black.

The parents of today's black children live in a different world. Educated blacks rarely live near poor, uneducated blacks. When these parents were growing up, the nation was committed to affirmative action, and many of them were able to go to college in record numbers, which resulted in a large, black middle class.

Many black children today attend schools that are crumbling and are not maintained satisfactorily. These children have many teachers who are incompetent, frightened and intimidated. The schools that these children attend have fewer resources, including textbooks. Yet they are expected to score well on standardized tests even though they have not been taught the material they are tested on.

Today the country is not committed to affirmative action and scores on standardized tests are the gateway to success. Years ago people who were high school dropouts or had only a high school diploma could earn a decent living. That was during the Industrial Age. Now we live in the Information Age, and the difference between having a high school diploma and a college degree is one million dollars over a lifetime. This will influence how your children will live and will affect the quality of your life as well. The sacrifices you make early on will pay huge dividends in the future.

This book is a guide to help you raise children who will be competitive in school and will have rewarding lives in the future. The following 50 points are suggestions for you to consider.

Contance F. Gipson

Wait until you can commit yourself to one woman before you have children. If you do not want to establish a family, don't have children at all. Even if your partner is using birth control, you should use birth control methods as well. This will save you thousands of dollars in the future. Some men have one to five children with more than one woman before they are married.

Parenting from a distance does not work. You will not have enough time or money to be there for all of your children. The women you want to be with may not want to spend their time and money on children you had before you met them. If you haven't settled down and you're fifty years old, recognize that you are not a prize package to many women. Look at the older men who have homes and are going on cruises. Generally these men are married. Many of the drifters are pushing shopping carts down the street!

*Parenting from a distance
does not work!*

Have children by the right woman. According to the United States Army, the most significant factor that determines a recruit's success is having an educated mother. Many men marry "down," marrying women who have less status and education than they have. Consider what this means if you dropped out of high school, have a high school diploma, or just a little college. This could mean that you are marrying a woman with little knowledge in the Information Age. If the mother of your children had her first child under the age of 20, her children are likely to enter school already disadvantaged. Children of teenagers are often low-weight children who will have difficulties in school.

The two factors that are predictors of children becoming criminals in the future are living in poverty and in single-parent households. (Levitt and Dubner, *Freakonomics*)

Try to marry an educated woman. Children who have a father with a limited education and an educated mother generally do better than children who an educated father and an uneducated mother. Successful children in school have mothers who read to them from the time they were toddlers. Ask yourself if your children were wanted by their mother. Unwanted children generally do not fare well in life. Ask yourself if their mother wanted children so that someone would love her. Steer away from teenagers who are trying to fill voids in their own lives.

For the sake of your children, try to marry an educated woman

If the mother of your children is a teenager, encourage her to give the children names that are easy to pronounce and are spelled correctly. This will give your children an advantage in the job market later on. Try to persuade her not to use overly creative names like Uneqque or brand names like Lexus or Alize. People with names that are common in low income black neighborhoods get fewer job interviews than people with traditional names. With many applicants to choose from, employers are reluctant to take a chance on someone who might embarrass the company. (Levitt and Dubner, *Freakonomics*).

Marry a woman who is sane. This seems obvious, right? However, fathering children with unbalanced women is all too common. Some women who may be different, exotic and exciting may not be wired well enough to make good decisions or to have orderly, stable lives. Women who lack common sense do not make good mothers.

Avoid marrying women who are unpredictable, unorganized, addicted to drugs or alcohol, who have loose morals or spend time trying to "beat the system." Avoid the person who has "learned helplessness." If you are attracted to women who can't take care of themselves, ask yourself if you have the Rescue Syndrome. Ask yourself if she could take care of your children if you died young. The woman you choose must be able to handle household accounts. Keeping her in the dark on fiscal matters can cause devastation in the future. It is better to make her your partner and to involve her in making financial decisions even if she wants to be uninvolved.

Unstable women do not make good mothers.

Choosing someone because you want children who are light and have "good hair" can be a recipe for disaster. If you marry a woman who doesn't like to read, didn't like school, and is poorly educated, your children will be at a disadvantage no matter how light or "cute" they are.

Focusing on inner beauty and education tends to pay off in the future. (By not marrying educated black women, black males may be leaving the first team on the bench!) If you marry "up" your chances for having successful children will be greater. Be supportive if she enrolls in college courses. You will benefit if she can compete with other women. Even if she will have more education than you, don't let your male ego get the best of you. It may take effort not to become jealous of your mate's knowledge and education, but you must remember that we are now in the Information Age, and you need all the information you can get.

Choose someone who is a caregiver and who will be supportive of your needs and those of your children. Beware of the "Princess" whose every need must be met first. Look for a person who can be depended upon to carry the load when you meet a rough spot in your career. Choose someone who can give as well as receive.

Focusing on inner beauty and education pays off in the future.

Be there for your wife when she is expecting your children, and be there when your children are born. You can try to prevent your children from having low birth weights by assisting your wife to stay away from drugs, alcohol and tobacco. Insist on her getting enough sleep and following the rules of good prenatal care.

Encourage your wife to breastfeed. Breast milk is the healthiest food your baby can receive because breastfed babies get sick less often. Breastfed babies tend to like a wider variety of foods later on. Not only that, you'll save hundreds of dollars by not having to buy formula and baby food.

Now is a good time to establish good eating habits in your home. Stress eating fruits and vegetables and healthy meals. Unless there are health concerns, avoid catering to children by letting each child eat different foods at every meal. Not only does this teach children that people will cater to them later in life, but this practice is time-consuming and expensive. You are not running a restaurant. Children should eat what the parents have decided will be served at each meal. They should try foods they don't like, and parents should make the decision on whether they should eat those foods. You can be the "health nut" in your home by establishing an exercise routine for members of the family.

Do more than your share in taking care of babies and doing household chores. Be affectionate towards your wife. Having babies is tiring and hard work.

Do more than your share
taking care of your babies.

Provide a stable environment. Put a roof over your family's head and don't move every time the rent is due. **Pay housing costs first!** Students who move often miss important lessons and tests. Be aware that most of the time students cannot "make it up." Students who move often sometimes end up without enough credits to finish high school. (One mother I know moved eleven times during her child's school years and then was shocked when he didn't have enough credits to graduate from high school).

If you are on your way to becoming financially successful, beware of false friends. Be aware that some people will not have your best interests at heart and some will not want you to succeed. Some "friends" and family members will not be above taking advantage of you financially. Keep all of your investments in your own name. True friends will not want you to spend money on them. You can remember where you came from without supporting half of your friends.

6 Provide A Stable Environment

It's honorable to help your friends and family members and to try to bring them along, but it's more honorable to help them acquire the education and skills they need to work for others or themselves. Some friends and family members can involve you in questionable events and can drain the resources you will need to take care of your family. You may have to leave some old friends, ideas and activities behind.

No matter how little you think you have, take time to make a will. Even record collections can turn out to be valuable.

Put your family ahead of your friends.

Help your wife meet her employment requirements. Pulling against her is not an option. Recognize that the more she earns, the more she helps you and your children in the end. The higher she rises, the more opportunities your children will have. They will meet more people who are successful; they will be able to live in better neighborhoods, and they will be in positions to attend better schools. Their success may lead to a better life for you in your later years.

*Encourage your wife if she is
reaching for higher goals in her career.*

If you owe money for child support, don't wait for the court to order you to pay: pay the money! This will have an impact on your relationship with your children and their mother. You will be appreciated for making the effort to pay even if you sometimes come up a little short. Your children will feel loved and valued and their mother will feel respected.

Just because you have moved on doesn't mean that your children have moved on. Don't abandon the children you had in previous relationships. They were yours first. They need your emotional and financial support. If at all possible, include them in the activities of your new family. Treat them as well as you treat the children you are living with now. Don't allow anyone to separate you from your children.

Paying child support will make your children feel loved.

9 Become Financially Literate

People who get a job, show up on time, follow directions and do what they are supposed to do are in a position to become highly paid. Let your children see that you try to over-deliver on every job you have.

Become financially literate. If your employer will match your contributions to a 401(k) or other retirement plans, go for it. Just because your great-grandfather, grandfather, and father did not believe in banks and put their savings under a mattress, you should not feel you have to hold on to this family tradition. Open a savings account and remember to pay yourself first. If you save small sums systematically you will end up with more money than those who try to get big money all at once. Many of the people who make big money illegally for a short period of time end up in prison making less than a dollar a day.

Teach your children that honesty pays and spending time trying to beat the system doesn't. Low level drug dealers have been found to make as little as $3.30 an hour (Levitt and Dubner, *Freakonomics*). They also have a 1-in-4 chance of being killed. (Levitt and Dubner, *Freakonomics*). Controlling a company is better than controlling a corner, a block or a few feet in a prison yard.

Establish a budget and pay your bills every month and on time. Let your children see you paying bills and have them help. Explain what bill pays for what utility, etc. Save some money every month. Don't waste money on a $500 birthday party for a two-year-old. Twelve-year-olds do not need five pairs of tennis shoes! Avoid spending large amounts of money on cell phone bills, coffee, lottery tickets, jewelry, recreation, rims, gold teeth, and cars. Having expensive rims on your car when there is no electricity in the house makes no sense. Some millionaires have never bought a new car.

Try to secure a loan from a bank rather than a sub prime lender. This will save you thousands of dollars and can make a difference in your ability to send your children to college. Keep your house looking good on the outside as well as the inside. This is your investment. When your house and yard are well maintained, you can sell at a higher price and use the equity for a nicer home. The two-step approach has worked for most people.

Pay attention to hazards. Too many black children die in fires. Buy smoke detectors for your home and practice methods of escape from fires. Make sure your home is free of lead paint and mold and get rid of unused refrigerators and cars near your home.

Controlling a company is better than controlling a street corner.

Teach your children to delay gratification. This means sacrificing now for things they want later. It means waiting until they have saved the money to get what they want and working hard in the present to get rewards that await them in the future. Set an example for them by waiting to buy things until you can afford them.

In 2004 about 29 percent of African Americans who bought or refinanced homes ended up with high-cost loans, compared to 15 percent of Latinos and 10 percent of white Americans. Some of this could be attributed to low FICO scores. Paying late fees does not help your credit score. People with a FICO score of 620-639 can pay $1,014 a month for a $250,000 mortgage while those with scores of 700-759 can pay only $874 a month. Try to get your FICO score up to 700, which most Americans have. You can do this by paying your bills on time and by paying credit cards with high interest rates down to zero.

Your children should see you waiting for the things you want. It is better to be rich than to be poor and trying to appear that you are rich.

Teach your children to wait for things they want.

Avoid overindulgence. Many parents don't want their children to suffer like they did because they were poor, but this is not reason to go overboard. Facing some hardships can build character. A too-easy life can rob a child of ambition and the ability to strive. Children who get everything they want don't learn that one can't always have everything one wants. They also have difficulty learning to overcome challenges and are less likely to become self-reliant.

Don't reward children for little accomplishments all the time. You want your children to feel a glow for doing well rather than working for material rewards. Keep rewards appropriate to what your child has done. Going to a D from an F does not merit a trip to Europe. A birthday gift for a 10- year-old should not be taking her friends to a mall in a limousine. You should not accept high cell phone bills and unnecessary spending from your children.

Graduation from high school should be the highlight of teen years, not the prom. Proms have begun to be more important than weddings and too much money can be spent on proms. Just because you can afford to spend a lot of money on your children doesn't mean you should. The money you waste can be put to better use in a college fund.

You want your children to love you, but they will not love you later on if they are not prepared to enter adulthood. Love in the form of overindulgence is detrimental to your relationship with your children and to their future.

Reward your child based on what they've done, not on what you can spend.

Establish an organized home. Children crave structure and routine. Too many black children live in unorganized homes that are filled with chaos. Teach your children to put things away when they are done and to do family chores. Setting the table and doing dishes is a good way to begin. Even young children can learn to dust furniture.

Too often family members are like isolates living in a home, passing each other from time to time. Each family member is in a different part of the house watching television and eating fast food. Eating together and telling each other what happened during the day is a must. If your work prevents you from eating dinner with your family every night, make sure you schedule time to eat with your family regularly.

You should be able to cook a nutritious meal. Yes, it's now manly to cook dinner. Try to eliminate fast foods. Obesity is shortening the lives of black children, and fast food is one of the main reasons. Plan family nights where the family cooks and eats together, plays a game or watches television.

Boys as well as girls need to know how to buy groceries, straighten up a house, scrub floors, do dishes and wash clothes. Expect your children to complete household chores in a satisfactory manner. However, treating your children like the help is not acceptable. Children are children. They should have responsibilities appropriate for children, not adults.

Establish family rituals and celebrations. Then you can say "In our house this is the way we do things. What other people do is not important."

Eating together and sharing your day with your family is a must!

Watch the health of your children. Set a time for bedtime and stick to it. Black children get less sleep than other children. Children 6-12 years of age should get 10-11 hours of sleep a night. Teens should sleep 9 ½ hours a night. A lack of sleep causes children to do less well academically and leads to behavior problems in school. Too many black children are up late, watching television, playing video games, talking to friends, or listening to music. Some parents are playing with their children late at night. Many children who do not get enough sleep put their heads on their desks and fall asleep in class. A lack of sleep can affect your children's health.

If your children seem tired all the time even though you think they are getting enough sleep, you need to find out if there is something wrong and to make sure they are checked by a physician. If they have special health needs, i.e. asthma or food allergies, make sure their schools are aware of them and have the necessary medicine available.

Don't forget dental health. Trips to the dentist are not the sole responsibility of mothers. Do your part to get your children to the dentist.

Overweight backpacks can cause muscle strain and back injuries. A loaded backpack should not weigh more than one-fifth of a child's weight . If you can, try to obtain a copy of the books your child is using at school for study at home.

If your children aren't getting enough sleep, they won't do well in school.

Watching television should be limited to one to two hours a night. The programs should be selected by the family. Television is a passive activity that does not require the brain to do much work.

Do not make watching television the reward for completing homework. This makes children rush through doing the work and makes television too important to your family. Recognize that black children watch far more television than children from other ethnic groups. Children from other ethnic groups are reading for pleasure and playing games.

Some experts feel toddlers who watch television more than two hours a day develop Attention Deficit Disorder. Four-year-olds who watch more than two hours of television a day are at greater risk of becoming bullies, obese, inattentive, and to show signs of aggression. You need to monitor what your child sees on television. Yes, some children can see lots of violence and sex on the screen and it doesn't affect them. But it does affect some children, so don't take the chance.

Don't put a television in the children's room and if you have, take it out. Most experts agree on this point. It's hard to monitor what they watch on television if it is in their room.

*Don't put a television in
your child's room.*

Love your children unconditionally and let them know it. Discipline your children as well. Girls, in particular, need love and attention from their fathers. Many who become teen mothers are seeking the love they did not get from their fathers. Many men who are in prison for murder had absent, uninvolved fathers. Avoid overly strict, harsh discipline but don't try to be the "good guy" at the expense of your children's mother. Women like nice men but they don't want men to be pushovers, either.

There is a middle ground. Yelling, screaming, and beatings are out, but you should have standards for how you want your children to behave. Even if you do not live with your children, you and their mother must be united on the expectations you have for your children. Be sure you back up the mother of your children if she is trying to discipline them fairly. Do not call your children demeaning names, punish them severely, or permit others to do so.

Praise is more effective than criticism. If you do not live with your children, resist the practice of having children assume adult roles when they are still children. Young boys should not be "the man of the house." Parents should be parents to their children, not friends. Children should speak to their mother respectfully and should obey her at all times. If you disagree with their mother, do it privately and try to work out a solution to problems.

*You need to set the standards
for how your children will behave.*

Carefully select the people you let into your children's world. Bringing people you barely know into their home is not a good idea. Pay attention to your male relatives but remember women can be abusers too. Children who are abused are often abused by grandparents, uncles, family friends, and church members. You may be in the best position to spot a potential abuser. Talk to your children about inappropriate touching and inform them they are to tell you if this occurs. Be careful of where your children are spending the night. Err on the side of protecting your children.

If you do not live with your children, limit the romantic partners who are exposed to your children. What you do with your partners is not their business, and they should not be exposed to your intimate affairs. Introduce only the people you have serious intentions of having a future relationship with to your children.

It is your responsibility to protect your children from abuse.

Introduce your child to the spiritual world. A background in the spiritual world may help them overcome obstacles later in life and keep them on the right path. Rituals and family traditions help keep children connected to their family when they are young and later in life. Going to Sunday school is not an out-dated idea.

Some people who take wrong turns in life eventually find their way back to the right track if they have a solid religious background. It's possible to raise children to be good people without exposing them to religion, but a religious background could be crucial if you passed away early in life.

Churches can play a major role in your child's future. They provide opportunities for children to recite speeches and poems, to sing in choirs and to be ushers. Children learn to relate to other people, develop poise, and to develop the ability to perform before audiences. These are activities that develop leadership and responsibility. Children learn how to be in charge, how to be on a team, how to respect elders, how to entertain and serve guests. They learn how to dress appropriately for different events. These are transferable skills that they may use in the future.

A solid religious background can help your children in the future.

Foster appreciation of people from all ethnic groups and encourage your children to participate in activities that bring together people from different backgrounds. Blacks who limit their contacts to blacks only are making a very serious mistake. Knowing whites and other minorities outside school and work gives one a more complete understanding of all human beings. Children become more comfortable with people from different groups when they realize that all people have problems and life is not easy for many people.

Set an example by letting your children see you interacting with men from other ethnic groups. Joining groups like the Kiwanis and Lions expands your contacts and can lead to opportunities you never knew existed.

Insist that your children treat others with respect no matter what their backgrounds are.

Set an example for your children by interacting with men from all ethnic groups.

Instill in your children that being black is a positive value. Constantly putting down black people and what they do can make children feel they are inferior and belong to a group of inferior people. They start to feel that they do not have what it takes to succeed. If you are ashamed of being black, your children will sense this. You can help your children by placing black art in your home and by reading stories about black children and heroes. Many black people who live in white suburbs make a conscious effort to develop a strong black identity in their children by attending black churches and by associating with black children's groups.

Going to family reunions is important. All children need to know who they are. This is particularly true if your children are bi-racial. Some blacks have declared themselves to be mixed-race people, hoping this will make them more acceptable and less likely to be discriminated against. This is delusional and can cause confusion and anxiety. Children who are very light and who have strong black identities do better because they can handle discrimination when it occurs. They don't deny it when they see it. Black students who reject other black students on college campuses can end up without a support system that will help them to survive.

Help your children to see that the Black American story of overcoming slavery and Jim Crow has been one of the most amazing accomplishments in the history of the world. If you can afford to visit Disneyland, you can afford to visit a black historical site, like a station on the Underground Railroad. Try to visit an historical site every year. Expose your children to the art, literature, and history of their people. Don't expect schools to teach the Black history your children should know. This is the job of black parents and the black community. Use books, educational television channels and the Internet. Make a game out of knowing black achievements and don't limit it to Black History Month. But it's a good idea to make an effort to do a big, fun family affair during this month.

*It's up to you to teach
your children Black history.*

Bullying, cursing, hitting others and using abusive language should not be tolerated at home or in school. And no child should deliberately try to frighten teachers.

Be aware that zero tolerance policies have had a negative effect on black students. School personnel now call in police to handle school problems more than they did in the past. Children have been arrested for minor offenses such as bringing scissors to school or pouring milk on the head of a classmate. This does not happen as often to white children. Many black students are not graduating from high school and have been denied high school diplomas for showing any kind of behavior that can be perceived as "aggressive." Black males with disabilities have a particularly hard time. Impress upon your children that they should be respectful at all times.

You can set an example by not ridiculing the color of your children's skin, hair or features. Do not allow labels, such as "the dark one", "the smart one", "the yellow one", "the no-good one", or "the fat one", to be applied to your children. Ban the word "n_____". There is no excuse for using it.

Bullying or using abusive language should not be tolerated at home or school.

Limit the time your children spend on entertainment, music, and sports. Have your children keep a record of how much time they spend talking on the telephone, hanging with friends, shopping at the mall, playing video games, playing basketball and listening to music. The time they spend on these things will probably surprise you.

Preview the movies you permit your children to see. Neither you nor the parents of your children's friends should buy tickets to R-rated movies for under-aged children.

Is the conversation in your home limited to sports and entertainment? You can change that if you want to, and you should. Your children learn what is important in the outside world from their parents. If you show them you are interested in reading, working on a project, fixing up your home, or listening to the news, they will learn there is more to life than just hanging out.

Encourage your children to play musical instruments. Playing music can be a source of pleasure all of their lives. Most of all, show that you enjoy spending time with them. Activities such as fishing and bowling together can build a treasure trove of lifetime memories that they will value in years ahead.

Don't let sports and entertainment be the only things you talk about.

Watch your grammar and diction. The world will judge your children on how they speak. Speakers of Black English are evaluated by some teachers as inferior to speakers of Standard English. This lowers the expectations they have of these children, leading them to pay less attention to them, demand less effort from them, provide them with less feedback and to call on them less often. They seat these children farther away from them, smile at them less often and wait less time for them to respond to questions.

First impressions matter. Some blacks feel they can switch from Black English to Standard English when the appropriate time comes. But this strategy has failed many black people. In the middle of a television interview they forget to put 's' on the end of words and say "I seen" instead of "I saw" and "He done" rather than "He did." Standard English takes practice. Unless you know your children will always be employed by blacks in the inner city, prepare your children by speaking Standard English in your home and insist they use it. They won't have to think about it when they need to use it.

Don't allow others to chastise your children for talking "white." Tell your children to help those who need help in speaking well.

Speaking Standard English will increase your children's chances of success.

Let your children see you read (not just the sports page). Reading is not just for girls and women. Your children's jobs will in all likelihood require reading. When black children enter school, they do less well than other children in matching pictures with words. Their parents have not spent time explaining what is going on in the world and talking to them. They have not had enough time using language because too many have parents who have told them to shut up.

Children must be encouraged to talk and ask questions. Poor families talk much less than affluent families. A 1995 study by the University of Alaska showed that babies in poor families heard about 600 spoken words per hour. Children in affluent homes heard an average of 2,100 words per hour. (Erika Chavez, *Sacramento Bee*, June 2, 2004)

Even if you never liked to read, don't say, "I don't like to read, either." Don't pass this on. Black children are not read to as much as other children. Dads should read to children, too. Ask them to tell you what is happening in the story at different times and ask them to predict what will happen next. Ask them to summarize the story. Work with them on words they do not know. Ask them to find information in a story and discuss it with you.

Discuss what is going on in the newspaper with your children. Talk to your children when you are out with them and explain what is happening in the world. They should not depend on luck or fate or adopt the philosophy that they have no control over their lives. It is your duty to let your children know that they have a place in the world and that they can affect what happens to them.

Let your children know they have the power to affect what happens to them.

Assume the responsibility for the education of your children. Send your children to school bathed, with clean clothes on, and well fed (watch the sugar). They should be in school every day they are not sick, and they should be on time every day. Teach your children that school is their job. It is their responsibility to learn. Stress that you are not sending them to school to have a good time talking to friends, gossiping, and wasting time in hallways. They should be in class listening to their teachers. If you find that they are wasting time in school, put a stop to it at once.

It is also your job to help them learn. Too many black parents believe that their responsibility ends when they send their children to school. They believe it is solely the responsibility of teachers to educate their children. It is not up to teachers to come to your house to help your children if they are falling behind. Much of what other children know comes from material they learned outside of school. Do not leave all the work to the women in your family. If your child is having trouble learning the multiplication tables, get a set of multiplication flash cards at a store. (Yes, you Dad!), Start with the 1's and ask your child to learn the answers and then come back to you to be tested. When they have mastered the 1's, send your child back to learn the 2's. Keep this up until your child has mastered all the facts. Not only will they learn multiplication but they will learn that learning is important to you. This can make a difference in their desire to achieve.

Remember, teachers do not have much time to work individually with children during class time. But you must make the time to help your children even if you are a busy person.

Help your children with their studies if they need it.

Provide a nice, well-lit place for doing homework and provide the supplies your children need to do the work. They should have a globe, dictionary, thesaurus and a computer. If you spend money on renting videos and games, you can afford a computer. If you absolutely cannot afford a computer, make arrangements for your children to use one at a library. When you were in school, this was not essential. **Today having a computer in the home is not a luxury. It is essential! Your child must know how to use the internet!**

Be sure to monitor what is happening on the computer. Trust, but verify. Tell your children about the dangers in chat rooms and predators. Take advantage of the safeguards that are available!

Make sure the place your children study is a quiet place. If they do homework in the kitchen, the television should not be on. Mom and Dad should be quiet. Keep distractions to a minimum.

Don't worry about overtaxing your child's brain. Asian students study 12 hours a week and white students study 10 hours a week. Black students study only 4 hours a week! Asian and white kids are not smarter, they just study more. In the years after slavery, many black people believed if people were too smart they were likely to go crazy. Some people today are helicopter parents who hover over their children, afraid that their children will become upset or suffer a loss if self esteem if they face something hard or study too long.

*Having a computer in your home
for your children is not a luxury.*

Stress rigor and working hard in school and on homework. Teach your children to use time wisely. Too many black parents want their children to play rather than learn. Children should be learning on weekends, too. Do not accept low grades from children who can do better, and don't blame others for their poor performance. Even if you do not live with your children, you should play an active part in their school experience. Fathers should attend parent conferences as well as mothers. You should see report cards, SAT-9 scores and other achievement scores. If you give the school self-addressed envelopes, they can send information to you directly.

Keep a record of your children's grades and display good report cards and good work in your home. Volunteering at school makes a big difference to children. They see the connection between school and home. Get to know your children's teachers and principal and visit their schools in a cooperative manner. Be positive about their schools and supportive of school personnel. If you feel some things are not right with your children's education, do not disparage the schools in front of your children but quietly seek to correct the situation. If all else fails, try to change schools.

Do not accept poor behavior from your children even if school personnel were at fault. Check with school officials to see if your children are engaged in any harmful behaviors. If they are, find out why and do what is necessary to change them.

Get to know your children's teachers
and volunteer at their school.

Teach your children that test scores matter. Too many black children doodle and daydream during standardized tests. Stress that they must always do their best. Tell them they must work hard to succeed in life. Don't say "These middle school scores don't count" or "They don't need all this stuff to get into college."

Scores do count in ways you haven't thought of. The National Achievement Scholarships for Outstanding Negro Students and National Merit Scholarships are based on eleventh grade Preliminary Scholastic Aptitude Test (PSAT) scores. Community colleges give scholarships that are based on high test scores. Encourage your children to take every test seriously if you care about their future.

Help your children to gain a body of knowledge. Learning facts is important and your children should be able to easily recall facts that are important. All children should have a solid background related to the culture of the United

States and the world. An excellent resource is *The Core Knowledge Series Resource Books for Kindergarten Through Grade Six*. This series by E. D. Hirsch, Jr. includes *What Your First Grader Needs to Know* through *What Your Sixth Grader Needs to Know*.

You can help your children by encouraging them to use their memorization skills. Memorizing poems, dates and facts can lead to higher test scores. You can also assist your children by buying games that rely on recalling trivia.

If you take school tests seriously your children will too.

Watch for grade inflation. Some teachers tend to give black students high grades for being nice and not causing trouble. Black girls, in particular, are sometimes rewarded for non-academic chores, like monitoring the classroom. Getting A's in remedial classes is not the same as being a straight A student in regular classes. Many parents of children who receive A's are surprised when standardized tests show their children are at the bottom of the class. Children must be able to face the fact that they are doing poorly in school.

If your child is not succeeding in the eighth grade, he or she may be in danger of failing the high school exit exam. Don't believe your child can become a successful high school student without getting some assistance. Don't say, "Well, they can make it up." They can, but only if you have a plan and take advantage of what other parents do when they children have problems. What do smart families do? They hire tutors. They use Kaplan books. They enroll their children in Sylvan or similar private courses. They don't regard summer school as punishment. They use summer school to improve the grades of their children. They don't regard repeating a grade as a stigma or punishment. And they don't wait until it is too late to intervene. They know that the knowledge their children gain will probably lead to better grades in the future.

Don't wait until your child scores below the proficient level to get help.

Be consistent and don't back off when your children make a little progress. Some parents are too satisfied with small progress. Students must pass the English Language/Arts and the Mathematics parts of the California high school exit exam before they can receive a diploma. Eighteen percent of all black students in the class of 2006 have not passed the English/Language Arts test. Twenty four percent have not passed the Mathematics test. This does not include the students who have already dropped out. A UCLA study has shown that the percentage of black students passing these tests is even lower.

High school graduates make $7000 a year more than non-graduates. Intervene as soon as possible to get your children on the right track. You can buy books at major book stores that you can use to help your children achieve in reading and mathematics. Children in grades 4-8 have improved their scores by using the Reader's Digest National Word Power Challenge, a nationwide vocabulary contest. This test helps children improve their vocabulary and helps them score higher on tests. You may enroll your children by calling 866-526-6388.

Stress excellence, not what's just good enough to get by. You can set an example by shunning short cuts to obtain your personal goals. Too many people move on before they are adequately prepared to take the next step. Let your children see that you believe in being thoroughly prepared for the goals you are trying to achieve.

Keep pushing if your children are not achieving as well as they could.

Teach your children time management, to pay attention to detail, to follow directions, and to follow through with work. Teach them how to make lists of things that need to be done. Have them cross off items that they have completed and compliment them for doing jobs, even if they aren't perfect.

Set a good example by showing up, keeping promises, and being on time. Ask yourself if you are always running late. If you are, make sure you don't do it when your children are involved.

When your children get a gift or someone does something special for them, require them to write thank you notes. This helps them to learn how to complete tasks and helps them to understand that they are not entitled to gifts and special favors.

*Set a good example by showing up
on time for your children.*

If your child is not doing well and is about to be placed in Special Education, make sure your child is tested properly. Many black children are dumped into Special Education for personality or conduct disorders. These problems may be related to learning disabilities or attention deficit hyperactivity disorder (ADHD), It may be necessary to have your child tested by an outside psychologist, preferably black and male, if your child is male. Become familiar with the resources that are available to your family. Make sure your child gets the right education and medical or psychological treatment that he or she needs.

Many black children, particularly males, do not do well when they have to sit still for long periods. The present practice of eliminating recess has made school less accommodating for black students because they cannot release energy as they once did. Try to find a school that is creative, has small group interaction between teachers and students, and has lessons that use oral language. It is amazing that some schools cannot capitalize on the creativity and the ability of some students to learn complex songs and poems outside of school.

Make sure your children are in the right classes for their needs.

Take advantage of every educational opportunity for your children. Be aware that gifted black students are reprimanded more than any other group in school. They are the most criticized and the least praised of any group. They are also the group that receives the least attention. These children are often subjected to unfair treatment due to subjective criteria, preventing them from receiving awards and honors. One valedictorian was not allowed to give a speech at his graduation because his dad had cut his hair too short.

Black students are disciplined for subjective infractions such as loitering and threats while white students are more likely to be disciplined for more clear-cut violations—smoking, obscene language, leaving school without permission, or vandalism. In other words white students are expelled for serious offenses while black students are more likely to be expelled or suspended for less serious offenses. (Center for Evaluation and Education Policy). Black students are 2.6 times as likely to be suspended as white students. This has been called the School-to-Prison Track. (Civil Rights Project at Harvard University). Don't let your child be pushed out of school.

If your child is labeled a troublemaker or is being treated unfairly, don't hesitate to select another school. If your child is suspended, expelled or has been incarcerated, try to get him or her re-enrolled in a regular school.

If your child is having trouble in school, you need to find out why.

Encourage your children to take advantage of school offerings, including activities they may feel are not "black." Black students do not participate in all their schools have to offer. For some this may be because they have family responsibilities. But many are just not aware of how much extra-curricular activities count when they want to go to college. Extra-curricular activities can pinpoint which careers they want to pursue. They should be encouraged to join debating teams, French and chess clubs, swim teams and newspapers staffs. Support them when they want to run for student government. It's not always where your children went to school, but what they did while they were there, when it comes to college admission.

Watch how many hours they work after school. Working after school can be beneficial but even good students should not work more than 20 hours a week during the school year. If they work long hours and make lots of money while their grades are going down, you haven't achieved what you want them to do.

Mathematics and science are essential for your children's future.

Monitor your children's activities when they are not in school. Latchkey kids should not be under 12 years old and should be required to check in with an adult every day. Know where your children are and who their friends are. Encourage your children to choose friends who have a positive attitude towards school, parents and your community. Most of your children's time is spent out of school. What they do in their free time makes a big difference in school achievement.

Having a library card is essential and going to the library regularly should be a must. Your children should be reading for recreation every week. Discuss the books they are reading with them. Building a home library is a good idea. You should spend more money on books and educational games than on expensive clothes, telephones and video toys. Some black homes have no reading material at all. Take your children to museums, concerts and plays. These activities are not things just mothers do. You need to participate in these kinds of activities as well.

When you are on your way to a family reunion, don't speed by Valley Forge, Gettysburg National Park, and the Grand Canyon. This is your children's country, and its heritage and beautiful sites should be important to them. It is your job to make sure that your children feel connected to their country.

Take your children to museums, plays and on trips to historic sites.

Teach your children how to work with others in a cooperative manner. Stress that envy and jealousy of others must be avoided.

Every tub must sit on its own bottom. Your children should not try to tear down others to build up their own self esteem. At the same time they must try to be respected by others. You do not want then to be passive human beings.

Do not ignore your children's reports of being bullied. Girls must be taught to walk with their heads up high and with their shoulders back. A timid walk invites bullies. Children can sometimes diffuse bullies by saying "Thanks for sharing," and walking away. Children must be taught that even if they feel they are being disrespected, harming another person is not the answer.

*Every tub must sit on
its own bottom.*

Assist your children in establishing goals for the future. Ask them what their goals are frequently, and help them to reach their goals. When you ask them what they want to be, don't accept "I don't know." Changing goals is better than having no goal at all. Help them to discover their interests and aptitudes by watching what they are interested in.

Fight the notion that people who succeed are just lucky or that things fell in their laps. Stress that people who get good grades are not just "naturally smart " but they study long hours. Do not accept negative attitudes about being smart, higher education, studying, reading, mathematics, and science. Stress black history and tell your children that being excellent and getting good grades has never been "acting white." When slavery ended almost four million blacks could not read or write. But they tried to learn in as many ways as they could. They did not believe that they were incapable of doing well.

Teach your children to respect the "nerds." Nerds often become bosses and having nerds as friends can lead to employment later on.

Be sure your children are following their dreams and not yours. Support them if they want to pursue careers that are nontraditional for their gender. Avoid damaging statements like, "You'll never be able to become a doctor." If you tend to put down your children, ask yourself if you are jealous of them.

Help your children
follow their dreams.

Insist that your children meet your academic standards before they are allowed to play sports. This will help them understand the consequences of poor performance.

If your children want to be professional athletes, don't discourage them but point out that the number of professional athletes is quite small. Insist that they have a Plan B and make sure that they meet the requirements to enter that career. Explain that colleges can choose athletes who have good grades, and they are reluctant to waste scholarships on athletes who will not be able to handle college work. Inform them that professional sports is a business and the careers of professional athletes can be short.

Set rules that make good grades the requirement for playing sports.

Encourage your children to go to college. Successful students usually knew that college was always in their future. Take your children to college fairs and to college campuses. Even those people who do not finish college still gain valuable knowledge, experience and contacts from attending college.

Recognize that working your way through college is not as easy as it once was. If you can help your child financially, do it. You may have been able to work your way through school years ago, and it can still be done, but it is harder today. Your children are up against people who study practically every waking hour. Grades in college count and working one's way through undergraduate school can have a negative impact on grades. This can affect your children's chances of getting a graduate degree, and a graduate degree today is like a bachelor's degree was years ago. Your children can work part time to help with expenses, but it isn't fair to think they can pay for college themselves if you can afford to vacation in Vail.

Don't tell your children that you can't afford to send them to college so they can't go. There are many ways that the lack of finances can be overcome. Become competent in financial aid.

Steer your children toward community colleges rather than private vocational schools. Private vocational schools promise placement in lucrative jobs and many are good. But many fail to live up to their promises and leave students with high loans to pay and facing bankruptcy before they even begin their working lives. Try to get your children to enroll in community colleges that offer the same courses at a fraction of the cost. If they are too scared to be on a college campus, walk with them on the campus and visit a class with them if you can.

Check your local fraternities and sororities about financial aid for your children.

Watch the classes to which your children are assigned. Algebra I is considered the gateway to higher education. Children who are college-bound should take Algebra I no later than the ninth grade. Black and Latino children are 30% more likely to be assigned to basic math even when they score as high as white students at the end of the seventh grade! Don't fall for the notion that they can be stars in lower math classes rather than going on to Algebra I. Students who remain in basic math rarely catch up with their peers.

It is better for your children to take the hardest classes they can handle rather ran watered-down courses. If they can handle Advanced Placement courses, encourage your children to take them even if they will be the only black student in the classes. This is not the time to show solidarity with black students who are not as capable. Preparation in AP classes can lead to scholarships which can save you thousands of dollars. However, children who cannot maintain a grade of B or higher in AP classes should change to the regular classes where they can earn an A. A grade lower that a B will hurt their over-all grade point average.

Many black students drop mathematics, foreign languages and science classes as soon as they can. Encourage your children to take science, foreign languages and mathematics as long as they can. Their options for careers will be greater than those students who dropped out of these classes. Today apprenticeship and technology courses for non-professionally bound students require a high degree of sophistication in mathematics and science. Try to get your children to take Algebra I, Geometry, Algebra II and Trigonometry before leaving high school.

Your children should be taking the hardest classes they can handle.

Don't rely completely on school counselors to tell you what your child will need to prepare for college. Counselors don't know everything. Do you own homework, especially about college requirements and scholarships.

Many black parents are unaware when PSAT and SAT tests are given. Don't wait for the school to inform you. Find out for yourself. It is not a waste of time or money for students to take these tests more than once. It is essential for students to become comfortable in a test-taking environment. Do not let your children's counselors tell you to let your children skip these tests.

Do not let your children listen to counselors who tell them they are not college material or they don't need certain classes to go to college. Do your own research with your children to find out what they will need to qualify for colleges and scholarships. If your child is planning to enter a community college before entering a four-year college, make sure the courses taken at the community college are transferable to the four-year college.

Do your own research to find out what classes your child needs for college.

Teach your children to stay away from drugs, alcohol, tobacco, gangs and sexual activity. Start discussions on the dangers of these things early. Do not permit them to wear gang colors and insignia. If you suspect any of these things are going on, confront your children in a calm manner and state that these things disappoint you and will not be tolerated. Do not permit them to go to activities where parents will not be present or with friends you do not know.

It is easy for teenagers to obtain alcohol. Some obtain alcohol from adults, an older relative, their parents, or the parents of other teens. Teenagers who consume alcohol are far more likely to die in car crashes. Don't be permissive about the use of alcohol. Get to know the parents of your children's friends. You need to know if they have the same values you have.

Some girls, even middle class girls, are attracted to boys or men who are "bad boys." Some of these men use alcohol and drugs. Girls who are involved with drug dealers are liable to serve time in prison. Do not permit your daughters to date males who are involved in drugs or who abuse alcohol. Girls should not be allowed to associate with males who are in gangs, no matter how much money they seem to have, how many presents they give, or how much they love them. Girls should be cautioned about having sex with "bad boys." Gang members, drug addicts, drug dealers and alcohol abusers do not make good fathers. Too often they end up in prison or dead, leaving girls to support children alone.

Discourage your children from associating with gang members. They should not be allowed to dress like gang members because they are likely to become guilty by association. To police officers, a person who looks like a gang member is a gang member. Stress that they may be harmed by mistaken identity if they "dress the part."

Start discussions on the dangers of drugs, alcohol, and gangs early.

There is no law that says that you should buy your children cars when they turn sixteen. Data show that owning and taking care of cars can make grades go down! Car crashes are still a leading cause of death for teenagers. Resist buying cars until your children are mature, if you feel the need to buy them at all. If you decide to buy your child a car, stick to good, reliable, heavy used cars. Inexperienced drivers do not need sports cars or the latest model.

Don't permit your children to drive other teenagers or to be passengers in cars driven by teenagers. Teenagers with passengers tend to drive over the speed limit or to tailgate. Teen drivers with a teen passenger have are twice as likely to have a crash than teenagers driving alone. With two of more passengers the risk is five times higher. (*Sacramento Bee*, August 27, 2005). Don't rely entirely on driver training. Make sure your children know the safety rules and how to maintain their cars. And be sure to remind them that speed kills.

*Your children should be mature
before they get a car.*

Educate your children about sex and the dangers of early sexual activity. Stress abstinence! But at the same time, educate them about sex. Don't expect them to learn what they need to know in school. Let your children know that you are willing to talk about sex with them and to answer their questions. Let them know that you will listen to them about their sexual experiences.

Data show that people have a greater risk of living in poverty if they have a child before the age of twenty. You should inform them about HIV/AIDS. Be sure your children know how to protect themselves from unwanted pregnancies and sexually transmitted diseases.

You can begin the sex education of your boys by teaching them that females are human beings who are equal to males. They are not objects whose purpose is to satisfy males. Teach them to respect the ideas of women and try to eliminate sex bias in their thinking about females. Stress that violence against females: hitting, pushing, shoving and verbal abuse are never acceptable.

Boys must be taught to control their sexual desires. They must be taught not to take advantage of girls, particularly those who are vulnerable or who are mentally handicapped. They must be taught to resist peer pressure to participate in gang rapes. Emphasize that "no" means "no."

If you are nervous or unsure how to raise the subject of sex, seek help. There are many resources that will teach you how to have "the talk" before you have to have it. Even if your parents never talked to you about sex, don't say, "Well, I turned out fine." You grew up in a different world. These days, with the Internet, video games, and movies, it's more important than ever that your children learn about sex from you.

Stress abstinence and inform your children how to protect themselves from unexpected pregnancies and sexually transmitted diseases.

Even if your life has been hampered by racial discrimination, don't allow your children to blame everything that goes wrong on racism. Remember that there are two sides to every story. Perhaps your child did not work hard enough on his assignment. Perhaps your child's paper did deserve a B+ instead of an A. It could be that the other child trying out for quarterback was better than your child. Perhaps your child was speeding when the policeman pulled him over.

Your children should be aware, however, that racism still exists. Although blacks and Latinos are stopped by police at the same rate as whites, their vehicles are searched and they have force used against them more often than whites. (Bureau of Justice Statistics, April, 2005)

Bias exists in health care as well. African Americans receive fewer mammograms, appendectomies, heart bypasses, and other life saving treatments than any other ethnic group. They receive fewer diagnostic tests for heart disease and diabetes. This causes African Americans to be more prone to illnesses, have more complications, and to die from illnesses at a young age, particularly asthma. (*Sacramento Bee*, August 18, 2005).

It is your job to help your children see racial bias and discrimination and how to cope with it. Teaching your children to believe that racism will never occur in the lives is not only unrealistic but dangerous. Some black children who are in denial about racism fall apart when it occurs. Others blame themselves unfairly when racism was the cause of the problem. Bi-racial children should be taught that they are black first. Running away from blackness doesn't work because society will always remind them that they are black.

Don't let your children view themselves as victims who cannot achieve because of racism, sexism, poverty or disability. These things can be overcome if they work hard and persist in trying to reach their goals.

Don't allow your children to blame every problem they have on racism, but make sure they know racism still exists.

Show respect for women. Provide an example of a loving relationship. Understand that your children will learn how to be in a relationship by watching you and will emulate your behavior. True, there are women who behave badly, but these women come from all ethnic groups. Most men go to great lengths to praise and to protect their women. Black men may be the only men in the world who denigrate their own women, their grandmothers, mothers, sisters, nieces and cousins in songs and poetry.

Teach your sons and daughters to respect women, and they will probably avoid pitfalls later in life. Don't approve of disrespectful terms that are applied to women and don't laugh at inappropriate jokes. Watch what your sons hear in barber shops. Do not encourage friends and acquaintances to push your children to think about romance. Early romances can lead to less attention to school work.

Encourage your daughters to wear clothing that is not suggestive. What they wear should garner respect from young men. Wearing suggestive clothing usually attract the wrong kind of males.

Provide an example of a loving relationship

Teach your children to respect adults. Talking back to any adult should not be tolerated, and adults should be answered in a respectful manner. Praise your children when they show good manners. Saying "thank you", "excuse me," and "please" are not old-fashioned. They are simply a way of showing respect for others.

Teach your children to respond to RSVP's (Please respond). Showing up when they have not responded is considered discourteous. Not showing up when they said they would is considered a lack of parental training. Good manners can carry a person far in life.

Teach young adults that they must show respect for elders who have endured racism in their lives. Respect must be paid to those who played major roles in the fight for civil rights. While the ideas of young adults for pursuing new strategies in this battle should be honored, those ideas should be presented in a respectful manner. Remind your children that they stand on the shoulders of those who went before them.

*Good manners can carry
a person very far in life.*

Insist that your children have respect for black people who are professionals, in position of authority, who have knowledge, and who are in charge. Many blacks feel that the members of their group can't possibly know what they are talking about and feel the knowledge other blacks have is suspect. They have internalized the feelings many whites have about black inferiority. Black children must learn to respect and rely on each other.

Dr. Benjamin Carson was chief of pediatric neurosurgery at Johns Hopkins by the age of thirty three. Most patients believed that he must have known what he was doing to have risen this far at such an early age. Dr. Carson said in *The Big Picture*, "I actually had more trouble earning the trust of some of my black patients. No sooner would I walk into the examination room than I would see the wheels starting to grind inside their minds...I could tell they were thinking, `I'm not going to have some affirmative action benefittee operate on the brain of my child.' They automatically assumed I had gotten my position not because I was qualified but because I helped meet some quota."

Asian students do well because they study in groups. Jewish, Asian and Latino business people help each other in business affairs. As a group, white males are unsurpassed when it comes to mentoring each other. Life will be much easier for black children if they help each other and learn to work toward common goals while they are young.

Black children must respect each other and rely on each other.

Teach your children how to handle an encounter with police. Tell them not to run away, be respectful, speak softly, and call police by their title, "Officer." They should be told not to raise their voices and not to argue with the police even if they feel they were stopped without reason. Your children should memorize the officer's name and badge number and ask for their parents to be contacted. They should not make any sudden moves. Tell your children to answer questions but to say as little as possible. They should not make confessions since anything they say can be held against them later on.

Children should be aware that some officers try to goad people into striking them in order to make an arrest. Children should never strke a police officer even if they are being provoked. (Stamper, *Breaking Rank: Top Cops Expose of the Dark Side of American Policing.*).

If your child appears to be on the wrong path, get professional help as soon as you can. The amount of money that can be lost in getting bail, paying lawyers, taking time off work for court appearances can be enormous. The money the black community collectively loses each year from these activities is staggering.

Spend time to help your children make up for the time they lost on court appearances and watered-down juvenile hall programs (Gardere, *Smart Parenting for African Americans*.)

Do not tell your children that all police officers are bad. Many spend countless hours working with children and are committed to fairness in the criminal justice system. If you can, get your children involved with the Police Athletic League (PAL). Knowing police officers may be beneficial to them in the future.

Teach your children to be respectful with police and to never strike a police officer.

Become involved with organizations in your community. Work with your community to insure that suspensions, expulsions and arrests are meted out fairly and for good cause. In 1998 black youths with no criminal records were six times, and Latino youth three times, more likely to be incarcerated than white youths for the same offences. (Civil Rights Project at Harvard University).

Black male organizations can teach young men to love and respect each other by bringing them together on a bi-monthly basis. They can teach young men how to work in a cooperative manner and can teach young men how to plan and execute events. If you do not belong to a black male organization, you can help to organize a group of young boys through your church. If you can, be a mentor to a young male who needs a positive role model in his life.

There are too few black male adults who are coaching Little League, Pop Warner, and soccer teams. Few black males who are good in sports are involved even though there are many opportunities for participation. More black men should volunteer to be tennis instructors, Boy Scout leaders, members of Big Brothers, and instructors at Boys and Girls clubs.

Black children need to learn how to win and how to lose. The more your children are involved, the greater the opportunity for them to learn these vital lessons. If you are involved, your children will feel proud of you. Other children will look up to you and will try to pattern their behavior after you. You can make a difference in the lives of the boys in your community.

You owe it to the children to work for fairness in your community.

Vote and encourage your friends and acquaintances to vote. Too many black men who are eligible to vote don't vote because they are too busy or uninterested. Black men believe that "they" are in charge and will take care of them. Black men cannot afford to be uninformed non-voters when a significant part of the armed forces are comprised of black young men and women.

Your children will be a part of the decision-making process in America. The actions of government agencies should not come as a surprise to them. The day has passed when blacks could allow themselves to be the last people to get information. Let your children know who represents them in local and state government and visit the halls of government with your children. Their lives may depend on it.

Don't try to get out of jury duty. The right for blacks to serve on juries had to be won in court by civil rights lawyers. Upper middle class whites are more than seven times more likely to serve than lower income blacks. If your child was accused of a crime or was a victim of a crime, you would want someone on the jury who looks like them. In order to secure fairness in the criminal justice system, if at all possible, **serve on juries.**

Black fathers need to teach their children how government works.

Afterword

In all the books on parenting, black men are invisible. It's as if you are not playing any role in the upbringing of your children. I know that is not true. Thousands of you are actively involved, sharing custody or are single parents raising children on your own. The media is rampant with stories about black men who left. This book recognizes those of you who have not left and who are trying to raise successful, confident children in today's world.

As important as it is for you to be there for your children, it is equally important to know when to let go and allow your children to stand on their own two feet. It can be more damaging to them if you continue to pay for their rent, utilities, clothing and food when they are capable to paying for these things themselves. You will feel justly proud when your children have entered the world as wonderful, self-sufficient adults who can contribute to the wealth and well-being of the family and the community.

Resources

Carson, Benjamin, M.D. *The Big Picture: Getting Perspective on What's Really Important in Life*. Grand Rapids, MI: Zondervan, 1999.

Carson, Benjamin, M. D. *Gifted Hands: The Ben Carson Story*. Grand Rapids, MI: Zondervan, 1990.

Clark, Reginald M. *Family Life and School Achievement: Why Poor Black Children Succeed or Fail*. Chicago: The University of Chicago Press, 1983

Delpit, Lisa. *Other People's Children: Cultural Conflict in the Classroom*. New York: The New Press, 1995.

Fereira, Linda, Tim Haag, and Jessica H. G. Schroeter. *Computers Don't Byte! Family and Kids Edition*. Westminster, CA: Teacher Created Materials, Inc., 2001.

Foster, Michele. *Black Teachers on Teaching*. New York: The New Press, 1997.

Gardere, Jeffrey, PH.D. *Smart Parenting for African Americans*. New York: Kensington Publishing Corp., 1999.

Hale, Janice E. *Learning While Black: Creating Educational Excellence for African American Children*. Baltimore, MD: The Johns Hopkins University Press, 2001.

Hirsch, E.D. Jr. *What Your First Grader Needs to Know* through *What Your Sixth Grader Needs to Know*. New York, NY, Dell Publishing, 1995-1998.

Holman, Sandy Lynne. *Grandpa, Is Everything Black Bad?* Davis, CA: The Culture Co-op, 1998.

Johnson, Ronald, and Constance Gipson. *Visions: Career Guidance and Life Management for African American Men*. Sacramento, CA: California Department of Education, 1998.

Latimer, Leah. *Higher Ground*. Columbus, MS: Genesis Press, Inc., 2004.

Levitt, Steven D. and Stephen J. Dubner. *Freakonomics*. New York: William Morrow, 2005.

Madhubuti, Haki. *Tough Notes:A Healing Call for Creating Exceptional Black Men*. Chicago: Third World Press., 2005.

Sanders, Nancy I. *A Kid's Guide to African American History*. Chicago Review Press, Inc., 2000.

Stamper, Norm. *Breaking Rank: A Top Cop's Exposé of the Dark Side of American Policing*. New York: Nation Books, 2005.

Wynn, Mychal. *Empowering African-American Males: Teaching, Parenting, and Mentoring Succuessful Black Males*. Marietta, GA: Rising Sun Publishing, 2005.

About The Author

Constance F. Gipson served as the Gender Equity Consultant for Vocational Education for the California Department of Education for over twenty years. She administered programs which promoted enrollment in nontraditional vocational education programs for men and women as well as programs for teen parents, single parents, single pregnant women and displaced homemakers.

Gipson is a national presenter and keynote speaker on school-to-work programs and has provided consultant services for state departments of education around the country. She co-authored *Visions*, authored *Visions Actitivity Guide,* and has produced several award winning video productions. She is also the author of *A Different Kind of Hero*, a three-volume collection of biographies of over 400 people, including many women and minorities who had an impact on American history.

Gipson has been actively involved in human rights issues for many years. She lives in Sacramento, California.

Kudos for The Black Man's Guide To Parenting

Constance Gipson has done a wonderful job providing a set of commonsense strategies, that unfortunately, are often not so common. Following her strategies should allow any father, or, for that matter, any parent, guardian, teacher, or mentor, to better enable and empower black children.

— Mychal Wynn, author of *Empowering African-American Males* and *Ten Steps to Helping Your Child Succeed in School*

I am the ninth of ten children in my family. My father died when I was four years old. I was raised by my mother and "The Village". Today, there is no "Village".

One of the reasons I founded the Continentals of Omega Boys & Girls Club in 1966 was to be of help from "The Village". **The Black Man's Guide to Parenting** *should be required reading for all males at an early age so that we can re-establish "The Village".*

— Philmore Graham, Founder, Continentals of Omega Boys & Girls Club, Vallejo, California

HOW TO ORDER
The Black Man's Guide To Parenting
By C.F. Gipson
can be ordered directly from Blue Point Books

VISA®/MASTERCARD® ORDERS CALL TOLL FREE:

1-800-858-1058

or visit our website at **www.BluePointBooks.com**

Each book is **$19.95**

For information about purchasing our books in quantity
for your company, school or organization, please contact:

Blue Point Books

P.O. Box 91347, Santa Barbara, CA 93190-1347

800-858-1028

fax: 805-687-0282 • e-mail: bpbooks@west.net